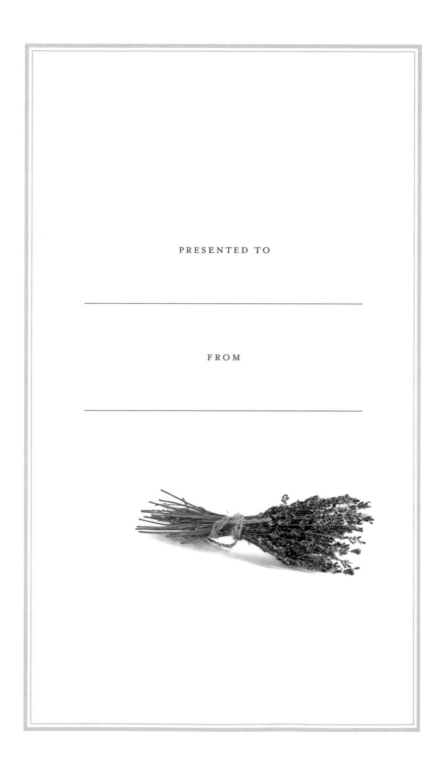

PRESENTED TO

_____

FROM

_____

A Mother's Gift of a Lifetime

my Mother
TOLD ME

INSPIRATIONAL JOURNAL

Bonnie Sparrman

"The measure of a woman's character

is not what she gets

from her ancestors;

but what she leaves her descendants."

ANONYMOUS

A Journal of
Your Life Story

Receive this book as a loving invitation to tell your family about your life. They are interested in knowing you. Let them see what shaped your life as you grew up, what influenced your decisions, and what is important to you now. This book is a gift for you, but even more, it is a treasure for your family to be cherished for years to come.

A s a child, I loved sitting at my grandparents' oak dining table listening to story after story of what we called "the olden days." Rules of etiquette and my mother's desire for us to know our history held us at attention when we were young. But as we grew up, we wanted to hear firsthand how our grandparents met, immigrated, weathered lean times, and built their lives on hard work and sturdy faith.

Our Great Aunt Lily, in particular, loved to reminisce. On summer evenings, seated on beautifully needlepointed chairs in her parlor, we listened to amazing tales of brave men and women who came to America in search of a better life. Her voice rose and fell in a pleasant melody, sketching vivid stories held fast by her sharp memory. What fortunate kids we were to sense the strength of our ancestors. Their bravery amazed us. We learned how they weathered tragedy and helped each other when times were tough. And what a thrill to realize how their stories intersect our own.

Each one of us has a story to tell. Into every life-journey God weaves amazing circumstances and beautiful patterns revealing his grace. Your story is worth telling. It is a gift to your children and to your children's children. As you allow this book to guide the telling of your particular life-story, remember that it is also God's story; worked out through the unique ways you are living your life.

As you pen your history on these pages, may you find joy in recollecting the gift of places you have been and the people with whom you have shared life. Often when we record an experience, more memories are unlocked. No matter your age or how much you remember, the reflections you share will be precious to your family. Don't worry if you need to leave some pages blank. Rather, enjoy the process of reminiscence knowing that your reflections are a wonderful gift for your loved ones. Let your personal story be the springboard that opens conversation about what it means to be not just a family...but your unique family. May you and your loved ones draw closer together as your story comes to life in *My Mother Told Me*.

Sept 13   Camp on...

the Junction

Marched 17 miles - Feel very lame an...

...up in morning. After g...

...about 3/4 of a mile to ge...

...make coffee - and then (ground o...

...stuff...

...thing...

...Passed through...

PHOTO

...ber in Pau...

...2 miles from...

...day. Marched very slow. Rested...

...also a couple of hours at Wa...

At dark the bugle sounded. Jal...

commenced falling - the men...

of marching at this hour of the day...

...meet with much approbation...

...bling about in the dark - trippin...

...who would blame the men...

...feel a little crusty. Besides the...

...be found - except - muddy - clayey - ste...

For you created my inmost being;
you knit me together in my mother's womb.
I praise you because I am fearfully
and wonderfully made.

PSALM 139:14

I was born on:
birthdate

I was born in:
birthplace

I was named:

I was given
this name
because:

BABY
PHOTO

My parents'
full names:

They were born:
birthdates and
birthplaces

My maternal
grandparents:
birthdates and
birthplaces

My paternal
grandparents:
birthdates and
birthplaces

My siblings
are: *birthdates and*
birthplaces

_____

_____

_____

_____

_____

_____

I am the _____
(first, second, etc...)
child in my
family

_____

_____

_____

_____

_____

_____

My place in
family birth
order influenced
my life by...

_____

_____

_____

_____

_____

_____

_____

_____

_____

FAMILY
PHOTO

A family is a place where

principles are hammered and honed

on the anvil of everyday living.

CHARLES SWINDOLL

The year I
was born, our
president was:
_____
_____
_____

My very first
home was:
_____
_____
_____
_____
_____

When I was a
little girl I liked
playing...
_____
_____
_____
_____
_____

As a child,
my bedroom
looked like...
_____
_____
_____
_____
_____
_____
_____
_____

16

I shared my
room with:
*(Tell what
that was like.)*

When I
looked out of
my bedroom
window I saw...

Sept. 13.   Camp on t...
                                tw. Junction
Marched 17 miles. Feel very lame an...
a heavy rain in morning. After g...
had to go about ¾ of a mile to g...
...make coffee — and then found...
...stuff ... that ... a m...
...water. ...

...14... ...in Cam...
PHOTO ... 2 miles from...
...Marched very slow. Re...
...for a couple of hours at War...
...dark the bugle sounded... fall...
...falling — the men can...
...of marching at this hour of the d...
meet with ... much approbation. ...
...mbling about in the dark — tripp...
...vines — who would blame the men...
feel a little crusty. Besides th...
...be found. Capt. ... muddy. slappy. st...

My best
memories of
being with
grandparents
are…

My
grandparents
taught me…

On rainy
days we…

On sunny
days we…

PHOTO
WITH
GRANDPARENTS

I am
immediately
transplanted
back to my
grandparents'
home when
I smell:

(How does this
make you feel?)

As a
preschooler,
I remember…

My mother
spent her days...
*(Did she go to
work or volunteer
outside your home?)*

My father's
work was...
*(What do you
remember about
your dad going
to work?)*

A picture book
that I enjoyed as
a small child was:

I liked to have
storybooks read
to me by:

The book
I requested most
frequently was:

As a child,
my favorite
color was:

Now
my favorite
color is:

This color
reminds
me of:

In the
summertime
our family
took trips to:

My family's
favorite vacation
destination was:

I liked it because:
(Were you with other
family members?
Cousins? What did
you do together?)

PHOTOS
FROM A
MEMORABLE
VACATION

27

When I was a
little girl, our
family car was a:

I especially
remember
driving to…

My family
attended
church at:

I was baptized/
dedicated at:
(place and date)

The pastor who
officiated was:

PHOTO
FROM
BAPTISM/
DEDICATION

My Godparents
or sponsors are:

Another
adult who
was especially
important to
me when
I was little:
(Tell why
that person was
special to you.)

My favorite
memories
of church
include...
(Tell why they
are special.)

My first
Bible was given
to me by...
(Tell how
it influenced
your life.)

Your Word is a lamp to my feet
and a light for my path.

PSALM 119:105

As a child,
my favorite
Bible verse was:

It was important
to me because...

As a child,
the church songs
I liked best were:

Your word, O Lord is eternal;
it stands firm in the heavens.
Your faithfulness continues through
all generations; you established
the earth and it endures.

PSALM 119:89-90

The first prayers
I remember
were...

I knew I was a
Christian when...
(When and where?
What were the
circumstances?)

The ways my
decision to
follow Christ
changed
my life are...

My faith was
nurtured by...

Sept 13   Camp out

Marched 17 miles. Tree very warm and

PHOTO

A childhood
illness I
remember
having was:

I was taken
care of by:

The worst part of
being sick was…

The best part of
being sick was…

I attended
elementary
school at:

I especially
remember…

My favorite
grade was:

I liked it
because…

ELEMENTARY
SCHOOL
PHOTOS

My favorite
subject in
elementary
school was:

_____

_____

_____

_____

_____

It was interesting
to me because…

_____

_____

_____

_____

_____

The subject I
found most
challenging as
an elementary
school student
was:

_____

_____

_____

_____

_____

I got through
it by…

_____

_____

_____

_____

_____

I attended
middle school at:

Something
I really liked
about middle
school was...

Something
I didn't like
about middle
school was...

MIDDLE
SCHOOL
PHOTOS

I attended high
school at:

My high school
was known for…

As I look back,
the teacher
I appreciate
the most is:

That teacher
influenced
my life by...

As a high school
student,
my favorite
book was:

I liked it
because...

Promise me you'll always remember:

You're braver than you believe,

and stronger than you seem,

and smarter than you think.

A.A. MILNE

As an adult,
the books I enjoy
the most are:
*(Tell what you like
about these books.)*

_____
_____
_____
_____
_____
_____
_____
_____
_____
_____

A poem or song
that has stuck
with me through
the years is:

_____
_____
_____
_____
_____
_____
_____
_____
_____
_____
_____
_____
_____
_____
_____
_____

As a schoolgirl, my extra-curricular activities included:

I chose them because…
(Tell what you learned through these activities and what you enjoyed or didn't enjoy about them.)

My favorite
after-school
snack was:

Jobs that I held
during high
school:

At home I had
some chores.
They were…

The chore
I liked doing
the least was…

The chore
I didn't mind
doing was…

The chores my
parents assigned
to me as a child
taught me...

As a child,
my family's
financial
situation
influenced my
life by...

When I was
a little girl,
my best
friend was:

Together we
would…

A friend loves at all times.

PROVERBS 17:17A

49

FAVORITE
BIRTHDAY
PHOTO

As a little girl, my favorite birthday celebration included...

A special birthday tradition in our family was...

As a child I
dreamed of
becoming a:

Over the years
that dream
changed...

As a girl,
my secret
hideout was:
(*Describe how it
looked and why it was
special.*)

The pets
I have loved
the most are:
(Name them and
tell why.)

PHOTOS
WITH
A PET

I went to summer
camp at:

My best
camp memories
include...

I learned
to ride a bike:

I used to ride…

My favorite
sports are:

Sports that
I played in high
school include:

TEAM PHOTO
OR
SPORTING
EVENT

57

One aspect
of my childhood
that I am most
grateful for is...

_____
_____
_____
_____

_____

My high school
best friends
included:

_____
_____
_____

_____

Together my
friends and I ...

_____
_____

_____

_____

_____

_____

_____

_____

Walking with a friend in the dark is better
than walking alone in the light.

HELEN KELLER

PHOTOS OF
HIGH SCHOOL
FRIENDS

When I was
a teenager,
a perfect summer
day was spent...

During high
school a popular
fashion was…

My most
embarrassing
moment in
high school was
when…

60 🦌

Movies that my
friends and I
enjoyed:

We liked them
because…

The time I got
into the worst
trouble was
when…

During high
school I
volunteered
for...

Some youthful
goals and
ambitions I was
able to fulfill
were...

I took music
lessons so I could
play the...
*(Share memories
of your teacher,
lessons and practice.
If you didn't get
to take lessons,
what was that like?)*

A concert, play, or musical that I participated in was:

You don't choose your family.

They are God's gift to you,

as you are to them.

DESMOND TUTU

My mom's best
home-cooked
meal was:

My dad's
specialty in the
kitchen was:

Our family's
table grace was:

This is how
my family sat
around the
dinner table...
*(Draw a diagram of
where you and your
family sat for meals.)*

draw a diagram
of your family table,
seating, etc.

Together,
my siblings and
I often enjoyed…

_____
_____
_____
_____
_____
_____
_____
_____

A special
memory of each
of my brothers
and sisters…

_____
_____
_____
_____
_____
_____
_____
_____

PHOTO
WITH
SIBLINGS

A joke that
kept our family
laughing for
years was...

A family
reunion that was
important to our
family was...
(*Where was it and
who attended? Share
a fond memory.*)

*The only rock I know that stays steady,
the only institution I know
that works is the family.*

LEE IACOCCA

71

My first date
was with:

We went to:

A formal dance
I particularly
remember from
high school or
college was...

I wore:

My date was:

PHOTO

The funniest
thing that
happened to me
on a date was
when…

My first kiss was…

The most
memorable
Valentine I ever
received was…

In high school, my favorite music groups or bands were:

The most unforgettable concert I ever attended was:
(Describe the experience.)

A favorite
hangout for
my friends
and me was:

My parents
thought…

My favorite
subject in high
school was:

I liked it
because…

I attended
college
or technical
school at:

My major was:

My decision
to choose this
course of study
was influenced
by...

During college
or technical
school, my
extracurricular
activities
included:
*(clubs, ministries,
hobbies, etc...)*

My first job
after college
or technical
school was:

_____

_____

_____

_____

_____

_____

The direction
of my career was
shaped by...

_____

_____

_____

_____

_____

_____

_____

_____

_____

_____

_____

_____

_____

_____

_____

_____

_____

_____

A talent that
God gave me and
I enjoy using is:

Through this
gift God allowed
me to…

Trust in the Lord with all your heart
and lean not on your own understanding.
In all your ways acknowledge him
and he will make your paths straight.

PROVERBS 3:5-6

BE STRONG AND COURAGEOUS.

Do not be terrified;

do not be discouraged,

for the Lord your God

will be with you

wherever you go.

JOSHUA 1:9

Some insights
from Scripture
that have guided
my life are…

My first trip by
airplane was:

I went with:

This trip was
noteworthy
because…

A mission trip
I took was…

Blessed are those who mourn,
for they shall be comforted.

MATTHEW 5:4

The saddest
day of my life
was when…

During sad
times I found
comfort in…

MEMORABLE
PHOTO

FAITH

is what makes
life bearable
with all its tragedies
and ambiguities,
and sudden startling joys.

MADELEINE L'ENGLE

PHOTO

When I was
growing up my
family celebrated
Thanksgiving
by...

My earliest
memory of
Christmas is...

To celebrate
Christmas,
my family
liked to…

A traditional
Christmas food
our family
enjoyed was:

The Recipe:
*(or attach
recipe card)*

My favorite
Christmas
carol is:
*(write out your
favorite portions)*

It is significant
to me because...

To me,
the most
important
aspect of
Christmas is…

Our family
celebrated the
Fourth of July
by…

As a child,
I thought
fireworks
were…

On Easter our
family...

For Easter
dinner we ate:

The holiday I
love the most is:
(Explain why.)

I learned from my grandmother,
    who grew up in devastating war times,
how important it is to keep with tradition
    and celebrate the holidays
    during tough times.

MARCUS SAMUELSSON

HOLIDAY
PHOTOS

PHOTO

I was taught
to drive by:
(*What do you
remember about it?*)

My first car
was a:

When I first
got my license
I liked to
drive to:

My family
member(s) who
served in the
military was:
*(What do you
know about their
experiences?)*

Books that
helped shape my
character the
most are...

99

When, where, and how I first met your dad:

On our first date we went to:

I was attracted to him because...

I knew he was the one for me when...

Our engagement
happened on:
*(Tell how he
proposed.)*

There is no more lovely,
    friendly and charming relationship,
    communion or company
than a good marriage.

MARTIN LUTHER

We were
married on:

Our wedding
day was…
*(Describe your
wedding day from
beginning to end.)*

The most
poignant
moment during
our wedding
ceremony was
when...

A wife of noble character who can find?
She is worth far more than rubies.
Her husband has full confidence in her
and lacks nothing of value.
She brings him good, not harm,
all the days of her life.

PROVERBS 31:10-12

103

Our wedding
vows were:

Scripture verses
that were read
at our wedding
were:

We took our
honeymoon to:

Our first home
as newlyweds
was:

A special
memory from
our first year
of marriage
was when…

The biggest
adjustment to
marriage was...

During the
early years of
marriage, our
faith was best
nurtured by...

The first church
we joined
as a married
couple was:

We were
involved with...
(A ministry, small
group, or...)

Other things may change us,

but we start and end

with the family.

ANTHONY BRANDT

Children are a heritage from the Lord.

PSALM 127:3

My most vivid
memory of
pregnancy was
when...

The children
who came into
our home:
*(Children's names
and their birthdates.)*

Share some
memories you
have about the
photos you've
attached:

BIRTH DAY
PHOTOS

As a young
mother I
loved to…

The biggest
lesson that
motherhood
taught me is…

As a mom
I felt very
blessed by…

The most
challenging
part of being
a mother is...

Some things
I wish I had
known when
I was younger:

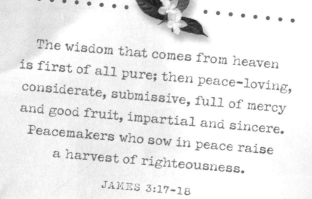

The wisdom that comes from heaven
is first of all pure; then peace-loving,
considerate, submissive, full of mercy
and good fruit, impartial and sincere.
Peacemakers who sow in peace raise
a harvest of righteousness.

JAMES 3:17-18

TRAVEL
PHOTOS

A man travels the world over

in search of what he needs

and returns home to find it.

GEORGE MOORE

The most
memorable trip
I ever took by
plane, train, or
boat was to:

The most
fascinating
place I have ever
visited was:

What I learned
about myself in
that place was…

A Bible verse
that has become
important
to me is:
*(Write it out
and tell why it is
special to you.)*

My favorite
hymns and songs
of praise are:

An important
time when the
Body of Christ
surrounded and
encouraged
me was...

Broad, wholesome, charitable views
of people and things cannot be acquired
by vegetating in one little corner
of the earth all one's lifetime.

MARK TWAIN

My most
treasured
possession is:

It is valuable to
me because...

An honor or
award that I
received was:
*(How did it make
you feel?)*

My confidence
grew when...

A recipe that
I am known for
making is:

It came from:

The Recipe:
(write the recipe or
attach recipe card)

A hobby or craft
that continues to
give me joy is:

If I could live
my life over I
would…

I would like my
children to know
that…

I would describe
my life as:

I sensed God's
hand guiding
my life especially
when...

When I consider
life's most
significant gifts I
think of...

A few more
thoughts I'd like
to share with my
family are:

For the Lord is good
and his faithfulness continues
through all generations.

PSALM 100:5

One piece of
advice I would
like to give my
family is:

When I
consider the
accomplishments
of my children,
I am most
grateful for...

When I
think of my
grandchildren
I am most
proud of...

A custom I
hope my family
continues is...

As I pray
for my family,
I ask God to...

One thing
I hope my
children and my
grandchildren
always remember
is that...

What can you do

to promote world peace?

Go home

and love your family.

MOTHER TERESA

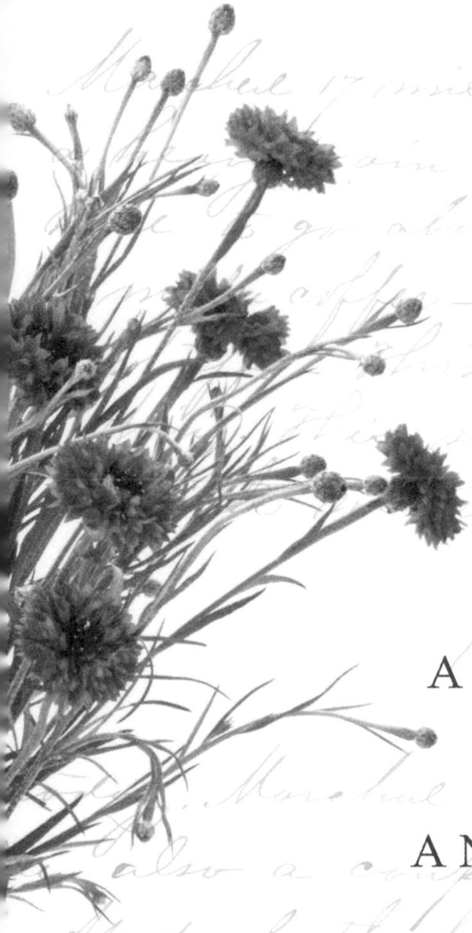

ADDITIONAL THOUGHTS AND PHOTOS

But seek first his kingdom
and his righteousness,
and all these things
will be given to you as well.

MATTHEW 6:33

My mother told me...

My Mother Told Me

Copyright © 2017 Bonnie Sparrman

Published by KPT Publishing
Minneapolis, Minnesota 55406
www.KPTPublishing.com

ISBN 978-1-944833-18-3

Design: Abeler Design, Minneapolis, MN.

First printing March 2017

10 9 8 7 6 5 4 3 2 1

Printed in the United States of America